Narcissism Decoded

How to Identify and Effectively Deal with the Narcissistic Personality Disorder in Your Relationship

By Michael Wright

Table of Contents

Introduction 5

Chapter 1: Characteristics of a Narcissist........................ 15

Chapter 2: Causes of Narcissistic Personality Disorder ... 47

Chapter 3: Problems and Difficulties of Living with a
Narcissist... 53

Chapter 4: Warning Signs.. 60

Chapter 5: How to Live with a Narcissist.......................... 76

Chapter 6: Managing and Treating Narcissistic Personality
Disorder 83

Conclusion 93

Introduction

Narcissism has been a recognized disorder since 1968 when it was first included in the fourth Diagnostic and Statistical Manual (or, DSM-IV). Before that, it had gone by the name megalomania. There are varying levels of severity but even in mild forms, it can be highly disruptive in relationships. So if you suspect you may be in a relationship with someone suffering from Narcissistic Personality Disorder, use this guide to help you figure out more about it and figure out how to manage it.

In this book you will get detailed information about:

➢ How Narcissistic Personality Disorder is diagnosed

➢ The characteristics of generalized Narcissistic Personality Disorder as well as its subtypes

- How to tell if you are living with a narcissist

- Common causes of Narcissistic Personality Disorder

- The problems and difficulties which can arise when in a relationship with a narcissist

- Some important warning signs that it may be time for you to get out of a toxic relationship with a narcissist

- Tips for living with a narcissist (when it is not yet too toxic)

- Potential treatments for Narcissistic Personality Disorder; and

- Important information about resources and advice for both people diagnosed with Narcissistic Personality Disorder and their loved ones

Diagnosing Narcissistic Personality Disorder

The DSM gives the following diagnostic criteria for identifying narcissistic personality disorder in a patient:

A. *Functional defects in personality defined by:*

    i.   ***Identity****: excessive reliance on others for self esteem and self definition; exaggerated self praise, either inflated or deflated (or vacillating between both extremes); inability to regulate emotions, often mirror oscillations in self esteem.*

    ii.   ***Self Direction****: Goals are based on obtaining the approval of others; sets unreasonably high standards for self so as to see oneself as exceptional; alternatively, standards are set too low because individual has a high sense of entitlement; usually not aware of personal motivations.*

AND

B. *Functional defects in interpersonal skills defined by:*

   i.   **Empathy:** *Decreased ability to identify with or recognize the needs or feelings of others; highly attuned to the reactions of others, however, only when it is thought to be relevant to self; either over or underestimates own influence on others.*

   ii. **Intimacy:** *Relationships are largely superficial and only exist to promote own self esteem; support and reciprocity are limited due to little genuine interest in the experiences of others and the predominant drive for personal gain.*

C. *Specific pathological traits may include the following:*

i. *Antagonism*

1. **Grandiosity:** *Heightened sense of entitlement; self-centeredness that is either overt or covert; strong belief that one is superior to others; often condescending.*

2. **Attention Seeking:** *abnormal attempts to attract or be the center of attention; constantly seeking admiration*

D. *Such defects in the function of personality and the individual's pathological traits are relatively consistent across time and situations.*

E. *The defects in the function of personality and the individual's pathological traits cannot be attributed to the individual's current developmental stage or social and cultural environment.*

F. The defects in the function of personality and the individual's pathological traits cannot be attributed to any physiological side-effects of a substance (such as drug abuse or medication).

To break this down into a usable definition, someone with narcissistic personality disorder is essentially someone who:

- Has an excessive need for validation from others in order to maintain his or her self esteem
- Gives him or herself exaggerated levels of praise or criticism
- Experiences extreme highs and lows in terms of mood
- Has an excessive need for the approval of others
- Sets unreasonably high standards for him or herself
- Has a strong sense of entitlement
- Has difficulty empathizing with others

- ➢ Has difficulty maintaining deep or meaningful relationships
- ➢ Acts very self-centered or egotistical
- ➢ Is often condescending
- ➢ Excessively seeks attention

The remaining criteria (C, D, and E in the DSM-V definition) simply point out that these symptoms should be chronic and disrupt the quality of the individual's life in order for them to be considered a personality disorder. It also takes into account the individual's age since younger people are much more likely to exhibit some of these symptoms due to the stage of development they are in. Finally, in the last criteria, it mentions that you should rule out the possibility that the symptoms are being caused by drug abuse, certain medications, or even a more general medical condition (such as head trauma).

Keeping these additional criteria in mind in addition to the characteristics listed above is important in accurately identifying narcissistic personality disorder. You want to be absolutely sure that the symptoms are not caused by any other problem because it is absolutely crucial that you are able to address the real root causes of these problems.

A Brief History of Narcissistic Personality Disorder

The origin of the term "narcissism" comes from the classical Greek myth of Narcissus, a man who became so infatuated with his own reflection that he died of grief after realizing he would never love someone else so much as he loved himself. The term has since been used to describe anyone who is particularly egotistical or vain. However, it was not until 1968 that narcissistic personality disorder was identified as a legitimate personality disorder.

It is estimated that approximately 1% of the population has some form of narcissistic personality disorder and it is slightly more common in men than it is in women.

According to Sigmund Freud, a certain degree of narcissism is a perfectly normal part of the human mind. It is this sense of love for oneself that drives our instinct for survival. In his theories of human development, Freud argues that between the ages of 2 and 4, as the child begins to develop a sense of self or an "ego," narcissism is a perfectly normal phenomenon.

Prior to this age, when the child is still an infant, it lacks a sense of self. That is, it lacks the ability to distinguish itself from the rest of the world; it has no ego. So when it begins to understand that there is a difference between self and everything else (around the age of 2), the child will behave in a characteristically narcissistic way.

This would not be classified as a personality disorder but a completely normal stage of development. Should this behavior persist into adulthood, however, it becomes a problem and can become very disruptive to the individual's happiness as well as the happiness of those around him or her.

Before moving on to the next chapter, it is important to keep in mind that you should avoid making any diagnosis yourself. If you think that your partner may be suffering from narcissistic personality disorder; be sure to get a professional opinion and diagnosis from an actual trained psychiatrist. This book is only meant to help you gain a better understanding of the disorder and the different ways to cope with it.

Chapter 1: Characteristics of a Narcissist

The diagnostic criteria given in the fifth Diagnostic and Statistical Manual were already discussed briefly in the introduction. However, it was quite a lot of information and it merits a deeper discussion to better understand exactly how a narcissist behaves.

The characteristics that will be discussed relate to the narcissistic personality disorder. While some of them may overlap with the normal phase of narcissism that occurs in childhood; the disorder differs in many important ways from that developmental stage.

Let's first go through each personality trait listed in the official criteria:

Identity

> ➤ *Excessive reference to others for self definition and self esteem regulation:*

This means that the person relies on affirmation from others in order to feel confident in him or herself. Behaviors like seeking the approval or admiration of others is counted under this criteria. A narcissist needs others to constantly validate his or her sense of self-importance. He or she may become very angry or depressed if that need for validation is not met. While everybody seeks a certain amount of validation from others in order to reaffirm their own sense of self; narcissists require an excessive amount. In some cases, they will need a near constant source of validation in order to maintain their strong ego.

➢ *Exaggerated self appraisal may be inflated or deflated or vacillate between extremes:*
Just as a narcissist will need excessive validation from others; he or she will also often excessively validate him or herself.

They will give themselves exaggerated praise and often judge themselves as exceptional or above other people.

Alternatively, a narcissist may experience extremely low self esteem (especially if they are not receiving the validation they seek from others). In this case it is also exaggeratedly low self esteem and is almost always related to a sense of entitlement. That is, the sense that he or she is owed something and until they get it, they feel they cannot achieve the exaggerated levels of accomplishment they believe they can achieve.

In many cases, a narcissist will shift back and forth between these extreme highs and lows. For this reason, narcissistic personality disorder can sometimes be mistaken for bipolar or borderline personality disorder.

➤ *Emotional regulation mirrors fluctuations in self esteem:*
Just as his or her sense of self esteem may fluctuate between extremes of high and low, so will his or her mood. When feeling, exaggeratedly confident, a narcissist will appear in great spirits: happy or excited—even to the extent of seeming manic.

On the other hand, when he or she is experiencing excessively low self esteem; his or her mood will correspondingly go down. During these times, a narcissist will seem severely depressed or even suicidal. Similar to what was described in the previous criteria, a narcissist will usually alternate between these two extremes of moods which can make it very difficult for the individual and other people to manage.

Self Direction

➢ *Goal setting is based on gaining approval from others:*
Because someone suffering from narcissistic personality disorder is so heavily dependent on validation received from others, he or she will often go to extremes to get this approval. His or her entire life could be based entirely around the need for this approval.

In many cases, simple approval may not be enough and a narcissist will seek to gain the complete admiration or envy of others. The goals set by a narcissist often will have little to do with any sense of personal interest or desire to accomplish them. He or she will only try to accomplish what is believed to gain the approval and admiration from the people around him or her. This could be anything from studying to become a doctor even though he or she has no real interest in it or attempting to impress others with athletic skills that he or she may or may not actually have.

➤ *Personal standards are unreasonably high in order to see one's self as exceptional or too low based on a sense of entitlement:*
A narcissist believes that they are inherently exceptional or special; anything he or she does is done well and comes naturally. This is not often, if ever, the reality. The difficulty or obstacles a narcissist might face in attempting to fulfill the sky high standards he or she has set for him or herself can lead to many problems including severe depression after failing to achieve these standards.

If personal standards are unreasonably low, it is usually because of a sense of entitlement. That is, the feeling that he or she is owed something. He or she may think that it is not important to try to achieve anything because this is the job of others who are below him or her. Narcissists of this kind will often feel that they deserve to be catered to and served by those around them.

➤ *Often unaware of own motivations:*
At the root of the problem of narcissism is not necessarily the high levels of confidence—almost always tipping over into arrogance. Rather, it is the complete lack of self awareness. A narcissist is completely unaware of his or her real self. This means they cannot accurately judge their own skills and limitations.

Furthermore, they are unable to understand their own motivation for doing things. When they set goals in order to gain approval; they often will not consciously know that they are doing so simply for that approval. They have little to no ability to know what they, themselves, might want or what would make them happy on a deeper, more permanent level. Instead, they pursue this unconscious drive toward external approval and validation; becoming instantly despondent and depressed when that external source of validation disappears.

Empathy

> *Impaired ability to recognize or identify with the feelings and needs of others:* One of the most difficult characteristics of a narcissist—that is, difficult for others to deal with—is his or her inability to empathize. They lack both the skill and the desire to put themselves in anyone else's shoes and try to understand how another person feels.

They also are not very good at satisfying

the needs of others. This lack of empathy is, at least in part, related to their own inability to accurately understand their own feelings and needs. Seeking only admiration and approval from others rather than real emotional connections has left them ill prepared to deal with the feelings and needs of other people.

➢ *Excessively attuned to reactions of others but only if perceived as relevant to self:* This characteristic is strongly related to the narcissistic need for approval and admiration from others. A narcissist can sometimes appear almost empathetic. However, upon closer analysis, you will realize that the moments in which they seem so empathetic, they are really just paying closer attention to how a person is reacting to him or herself.

Being attuned to the reactions of others is an important way in which a narcissist can notice if they are getting the approval or admiration they seek. Because they are so preoccupied with how others see them; they have become very good at picking up on every little cue that could indicate how another person feels toward him or her.

➢ *Over- or underestimate of own effect on others:*
While they may have a strong talent for picking up on even the smallest clues as to how a person has reacted to something he or she has done; narcissists are surprisingly bad at accurately measuring their real effect on others.

For example, they may pick up on a subtle cue that could be seen as admiration and overestimate how much influence they have over the person. Alternatively, any slightest indication of disappointment or disapproval could be exaggerated into a belief that they are entirely powerless over others.

Intimacy

➢ *Relationships largely superficial and exist to serve self esteem regulation:* Narcissists are notoriously bad at becoming truly intimate with another person. They will often have difficulty committing to another person and prefer, instead, to maintain a large number of superficial relationships rather than a few, deeply-gratifying intimate relationships.

A narcissist's relationships with others are used only as a means of gaining the approval they desire. There is little to no actual emotional investment on the part of a narcissist in the relationship. As a result, he or she may often stray outside of a committed relationship and have affairs. But there will be no emotional investment in any of these affairs, either. They would simply be for the purpose of obtaining the extremely high levels of validation a narcissist requires.

➢ *Mutuality constrained by little genuine interest in others' experiences:*
Someone who is in a relationship with a narcissist will often feel that he or she is putting much more effort into the relationship than his or her partner. This is because—if your partner is a narcissist—you really are putting more effort into developing a real, meaningful relationship while the narcissistic partner seeks nothing below a surface interaction.

Furthermore, a narcissist can be extremely demanding, requiring more attention and more validation than usual. It will feel like they are demanding an unrealistic amount from their partner while the partner receives little in return.

➢ *Predominance of a need for personal gain:*
The primary reason narcissists have difficulty with intimacy is that they show no genuine interest in others. Their motive for becoming involved in any kind of relationship—including friendship—is selfish. Relationships are a means to an end for a narcissist. If they cannot see any route to personal gain in a relationship, they will not expend any effort on it at all. In addition, as soon as they perceive that a certain relationship no longer serves any self interested purpose, they will abandon it or, at least, stop putting any effort into it whatsoever.

Grandiosity

➢ *Feelings of entitlement, either overt or covert self-centeredness:*

In addition to feeling exaggeratedly special or unique, a narcissist will feel an unreasonable sense of entitlement. In a relationship, they may expect a lot from the partner and feel completely entitled to all of it without putting any effort into the relationship or giving back to the partner in anyway.

In most situations, they will act very self-centered and believe that they are owed everything they desire. They will attempt to justify this sense of entitlement but, in reality, it will be largely unfounded or, at least, exaggerated.

➢ *Firmly holding to the belief that one is better than others:*
This is where the excessive arrogance characteristic of a narcissist comes in. He or she will often believe that no one else is as smart, athletic, successful or whatever other quality from which he or she derives

a sense of superiority.

It is crucial to the maintenance of the narcissistic world view that he or she be superior to all others. Whether or not this is true—and it rarely is true—is irrelevant since the narcissist also lacks the ability to be self aware, as discussed earlier, and cannot accurately measure how much better or worse he or she really is in comparison to anyone else.

➤ *Condescending toward others:*
Because a narcissist will often feel so much more superior than others, he or she will often act in a condescending manner toward them. Talking down to them, being patronizing, or being unnecessarily critical are common behaviors of a narcissist.

For someone in a relationship with a narcissist, this become a major source of strife as the partner perpetually puts his or her needs above your own and then criticizes or demeans you when you attempt to address the issue.

Attention Seeking

➢ *Excessive attempts to attract and be the focus of the attraction of others:*
In order to get the validation they require, narcissists will go to great lengths in order to attract the attention of others. They feel a constant need to be at the center of attention and become jealous or envious if the attention is taken away from them.

Narcissists will also often act excessively flirtatious or seductive and put a large amount of effort into their appearance in order to be regarded as attractive by others. Because of this, they are very bad at handling rejection or criticism of any kind.

> *Admiration seeking:*
> As mentioned earlier, narcissists thrive on
> admiration. They will put a lot of effort
> into getting the admiration they are after.
> They will resort to just about any means
> necessary in order to feel admired by
> others. This makes them extremely
> competitive which is particularly
> dangerous when combined with their lack
> of concern for anyone else's wellbeing.
> They will manipulate, use, or put down
> anyone they feel they need to in order to
> gain the admiration of others. This
> characteristic can also make them act
> quite impulsively; doing whatever strikes
> them as a way to be admired regardless of
> any risks or consequences involved.

**The 5 Subtypes of Narcissistic Personality
Disorder**

Within the broader category of narcissistic personality disorder, five subtypes were identified by a psychologist named Theodore Millon. Those five subtypes are unprincipled narcissist, amorous narcissist, compensatory narcissist, elitist narcissist, and fanatic narcissist. Each subtype fulfills the diagnostic criteria for generalized narcissistic personality disorder discussed above. However, they differ in which traits are most extreme as well as how those traits are expressed. In this section, you will get a brief description what characterizes each of these five subtypes.

Unprincipled Narcissist

The unprincipled narcissist has an exceptional amount of difficulty with empathy and intimacy. They have characteristics of antisocial personality disorder. Millon described this type as having a deficient conscience and being deceptive or exploitative.

They tend to lie a lot without concern for the consequences. They are disloyal, arrogant, and vindictive. They often have a dominant personality and can, therefore, be extremely stubborn and unwilling to make any sort of compromise. An unprincipled narcissist shows little sense of morality and has difficulties determining the difference between right and wrong.

For these reasons, they can become very dangerous people if their disorder is not treated or managed.

Amorous Narcissist

These types of narcissists are the charmers. They put great effort into being extremely sexually seductive and enticing. They are great at appearing clever and witty even if they have to resort to lying and manipulation. Amorous narcissists have a talent for attracting people to them as they have an almost bewitching personality.

However, they are incapable of engaging in real intimacy and have little concern for the pain or consequences that might occur from their seduction. They will often have affairs outside of a relationship and they have no respect for the boundaries of other relationships, sleeping with married or unavailable people without guilt.

The danger of amorous narcissists lies in their ability to manipulate and attract people to them. They can build up quite a following and manipulate people into doing things they might not otherwise do. An amorous narcissist might seduce or entice you into doing something against your moral code and then abandon you, leaving you to suffer both the guilt and consequences of the deed on your own.

Compensatory Narcissist

A compensatory narcissist differs from the other subtypes in that they often have deep rooted feelings of inferiority rather than superiority and seek to overcompensate for those feelings by creating the illusion of superiority and self confidence.

They operate on the belief that, if they can convince others of their self worth and exceptional value, it will alleviate the excessively low self esteem he or she feels. Compensatory narcissists will often act passive-aggressively and show signs of avoidant personality disorder such as hypersensitivity, mistrust or the reliance on fantasy as a means of escaping the painful feelings of inferiority.

Compensatory narcissists are not as immediately dangerous as the other subtypes but they can still cause a lot of pain especially as they attempt to distance themselves emotionally from others or act passive-aggressively.

Elitist Narcissist

The elitist narcissist—sometimes referred to as the phallic narcissist—feels an exaggerated sense of privilege or empowerment. This type of narcissist is particularly prone to feeling an excessive sense of entitlement and will demand special status, favors, or reward by virtue of the accomplishments or heightened social position they believe themselves to have.

It is closely related to the generalized form of narcissistic personality disorder. They feel an exaggerated sense of pride despite having accomplished very little of note. Rather than attempting to earn those things he or she feels entitled to; he or she will attempt to manipulate others or obtain them by associating with those people who would be able to offer it to them.

Fanatic Narcissist

Like the compensatory narcissist, the fanatic narcissist is battling with extremely low levels of self-esteem. The difference here is that they have a contradicting set of exaggerated personal standards. They often expect near omnipotence of themselves while struggling with an utter lack of self esteem at the same time. These two illusions pulling in opposite directions often lead the person to display traits of paranoid personality disorder such as delusions, paranoia, and disorganized thinking.

In order to compensate for their low self esteem, they will resort to fantasies and delusions of heroism and greatness. However, even in the midst of living out these fantasies, they are struggling to fight off equally delusional perceptions of their inferiority or lack of self worth.

Fanatic narcissists are not as often a danger to others so much as they are to themselves. The constant struggle between delusions of worthlessness and omnipotence can lead to severe depression and even suicide. The paranoia that they experience can make treatment very difficult or even wholly ineffective.

Are You Living with a Narcissist?

You have just read a lot of information about narcissistic personality disorder including the different subtypes that are contained within it. While reading through the diagnostic criteria and descriptions, you surely were thinking of who in your life might fulfill these criteria. But all that information is still a little abstract and it can be difficult to make a proper evaluation without knowing concrete examples of how these personality traits are expressed in everyday situations. For this reason, you will now have the option to take a short quiz to help you determine whether your partner might have a form of narcissistic personality disorder.

Again it is important to mention that this quiz should not be understood as a real diagnosis. For that, you need to consult a certified and trained psychiatrist—preferably one who specializes in narcissistic personality disorder. Use this quiz only for your own personal information and to help you decide whether or not narcissistic personality disorder could be a probable cause of the struggles you are dealing with in your relationship.

1. How does your partner react to criticism?
   a. He or she might sometimes become upset but, ultimately, accepts the criticism without overreacting. (1 point)
   b. He or she becomes immediately enraged and intolerant. (2 points)
   c. He or she seems to feel an unnecessarily strong amount of shame or humiliation. (3 points)
2. How does your partner treat you and others (generally speaking)?

a. He or she can be very manipulative when he or she wants to be. I have witnessed or personally experienced moments of exploitation (emotional or physical). (2 points)

b. He or she generally tries to treat people with respect and takes their feelings into account even if he or she might occasionally act as if his or her feelings are more important. (1 point)

c. He or she has a lot of difficulty with trust and will sometimes act very emotionally distant. (3 points)

3. How does your partner perceive him or herself?

a. It depends. Some days, he or she is on top of the world while other days he or she is just down in the dumps. (3 points)

b. He or she is generally confident. Of course, he or she has bad days but always recovers and seems very self aware. (1 point)

c. He or she is extremely confident; perhaps, too confident. Sometimes it feels like he or she has no respect for me because of how inflated his or her own ego is. (2 points)

4. What are your partner's expectations of you?

a. We have a give and take relationship. We both try to put equal effort into it and appreciate the other person's needs and desires. (1 point)

b. He or she has very high expectations of me and demands quite a lot without wanting to give anything in return. (2 points)

c. He or she can be very demanding but the main problem is that he or she becomes easily jealous or distrustful. (3 points)

5. Does your partner confide fully to you?

a. He or she seems to have trouble opening up to me about his or her feelings. I can see that he or she struggles with something but is reluctant to tell me what it is. (3 points)

b. We can tell each other everything and I know he or she does not hesitate to open up to me. (1 point)

c. He or she does not really confide in me at all about emotional issues and often does not even seem to feel emotions at all. (2 points)

6. Does your partner fantasize or obsess a lot about things like unlimited success, intelligence, physical attractiveness, or power?

a. Yes (2 points)

b. No (1 point)

7. Does your partner require what you consider to be an abnormal level of attention and become jealous or upset if

you do not pay as much attention to them as they want?

    a. Yes (2 points)

    b. No (1 point)

8. How does your partner react when you tell him or her about your feelings or what happened during your day?

    a. He or she expresses interest in how I feel and even when I talk about something I know he or she is not really interested in, I still feel that my voice is being heard. (1 point)

    b. He or she seems bored or annoyed when I try to talk about my day or bring up specific issues I am dealing with. At the same time, he or she expects me to give my undivided attention when he or she talks about him or herself. (2 points)

    c. Sometimes he or she will try to listen but it doesn't seem genuine. Other times, he or she becomes so emotionally distant, I feel as if I am living with a stranger. (3 points)

Quiz Results

- *8-12 Points: Not a Narcissist.* If you scored within this point range, congratulations! Your partner is almost certainly not a narcissist. If you still feel that there are some deep rooted issues in your relationship, try opening up and discussing these issues in a calm and understanding manner. Since your partner is likely not suffering from narcissistic personality disorder, he or she will probably be receptive to your attempts to discuss the relationship. If not, you may want to try seeking couples counseling.

- *13-18: A Narcissist.* If you scored within this point range, your partner could be a narcissist. Furthermore, it is likely that he or she is of the unprincipled, amorous, or elitist subtype. These types of narcissists can be extremely difficult—and even dangerous—to live with. Be sure to read the chapter about warning signs to find out if your relationship is too toxic to risk staying. Find out if your partner would be willing to talk with a psychiatrist and get an official diagnosis (and, potentially, treatment). But do so carefully. Narcissists will probably not respond well to being considered mentally ill.

- *19-22: A Narcissist.* If you scored within this point range, your partner could also be a narcissist. However, it is more likely that they are of the compensatory or fanatic type than the others mentioned above. These types are certainly difficult to live with but not as dangerous as the others. You may be able to salvage the relationship if your partner is willing to get help and work with you to manage this personality disorder. Of course, you should still be very careful in how you approach the issue with your partner. They will be very sensitive to being considered mentally ill and may easily take it as a criticism or insult. Be sure to read the section on how to live with a narcissist in order to learn how to best deal with the issue.

If you scored in either of the last two ranges, you may want to strongly consider seeking out a psychiatrist to get a professional opinion and find out what steps you need to take in order to either help your partner recover from narcissistic personality disorder or cut ties with him or her entirely before you risk being put in serious danger.

Chapter 2: Causes of Narcissistic Personality Disorder

In this chapter, you will learn about some of the causes of narcissistic personality disorder. The specific causes differ for each individual. But, perhaps, by understanding some of the general factors that can contribute to the disorder; you will better be able to identify what might be the root cause of the disorder in your partner (if he or she does, indeed, have narcissistic personality disorder).

While there is still comparatively little known about the exact causes of narcissistic personality disorder, a variety of potential contributing factors have been identified. In 2006, Leonard Groopman and Arnold Cooper put together the following list:

> ➤ Hypersensitivity originating at birth: some people are just more sensitive than others from the day they are born. Hypersensitivity can lead to an inability to

cope healthily with criticism or failure, leading to the need to overcompensate or set unrealistic standards for oneself in order to overcome feelings of inadequacy.

➢ Excessive praise during childhood: while it is, of course, important to praise your child for good behavior to encourage them to continue such behavior; too much praise can lead to an exaggerated sense of self worth. The popular parenting movement of the 1990s and early 2000s that sought to make every child feel special has led to an increase in cases of narcissistic personality disorder as those children who are now adults were raised to believe they were exceptional and superior to all others.

➢ Excessive criticism during childhood: Just as with excessive praise, excessive criticism can lead to the need for overcompensation in order to recover lost self esteem. Parents who are overly harsh with their children when they do something bad or fail at something risk raising a child that battles feelings of inferiority. This can result in compensatory or fanatic narcissism or a variety of other personality disorders.

➢ Overindulgence by parents during childhood: That is, parents who spoil their children risk raising up a child who will later develop narcissistic personality disorder. This is because overindulging a child's every wish and desire will give them the inaccurate perception that they are entitled to everything they want.

➢ Severe emotional abuse in childhood: Emotional abuse is, unfortunately, an often overlooked factor by society. We take great pains as a society to prevent physical abuse but have few options for children who are being emotionally abused. However, emotional abuse takes a huge toll on the psyche and can lead to a wide variety of personality disorders later in life including narcissistic personality disorder.

- Unstable or unreliable care giving from parents: children of broken homes or of unreliable parents grow up without that feeling of security and safety that is necessary for a child to develop healthily and become a confident (but not too confident) adult capable of achieving real happiness in life.

- A narcissistic parent: This is a factor not necessarily because narcissism is hereditary but because the child grows up watching and learning from how its parents behave. If the child witnesses the manipulative and self-centered behaviors characteristic of a narcissist, it will learn to adopt those behaviors.

- Abnormality in the brain: recent research has suggested that there may be actual brain abnormalities associated with narcissistic personality disorder. Specifically, those who have the disorder tend to have less gray matter in the left anterior insula. This region of the brain is thought to be responsible for empathy and compassion as well as for regulating our emotional responses. With this region underdeveloped, people have difficulties performing all of these important brain functions. The causes of this abnormality are still unknown.

Whatever the original origins of the disorder, narcissism is deeply rooted in a sense of shame and inferiority. These feelings are so deeply rooted, however, that someone with narcissistic personality disorder would never admit to feeling them—primarily because they are, themselves, completely unaware of these feelings.

At a subconscious level, every narcissist feels that they are fundamentally flawed in such a way that they are completely unacceptable or unsuited for normal society. This is why they deal so poorly with criticism, disagreements, or setbacks. Even if they are wonderfully ambitious and capable individuals, the slightest setback could throw them entirely off track; making it difficult for them to follow through or achieve long term goals.

The behaviors associated with narcissistic personality disorder, then, are defense mechanisms the individual has developed to cope with these feelings of shame and inferiority. This is an important thing to understand as you attempt to help your partner deal with his or her narcissistic personality disorder.

Chapter 3: Problems and Difficulties of Living with a Narcissist

There are many problems which can come up if you are in a relationship with someone who suffers from narcissistic personality disorder, particularly if it is a severe form. Learning more about what sort of problems typically arise when living with a narcissist will help you to better identify whether or not your partner is a narcissist.

Common Problems

> ➤ Unequal investment in the relationship: if your partner is a narcissist, they will likely be unwilling or unable to invest as much in the relationship as you do. They will act ambivalent about the quality of the relationship and their role in maintaining it. This becomes problematic when you feel as if you are doing all the work to keep the relationship together while your

partner carries on as if it is not their concern.

➤ Unrealistic demands: a narcissistic partner will often expect a lot more from you than they expect of themselves when it comes to the relationship. He or she will require a lot of attention and constant validation but fail to give you the same in return. It can take a huge emotional toll on you to constantly be supportive and caring for a person who acts as if they could not care less about your well being. You might find yourself emotionally exhausted from trying to meet the unrealistic demands that your partner has set for you.

➤ Distrust and jealousy: particularly with compensatory and fanatic narcissists, you may have to deal with an excessive amount of jealousy and distrust. The feelings of inferiority that lie at the core of a narcissist's psyche cause them to feel inadequate and even paranoid. This can lead to your partner becoming jealous over trivial things or distrusting you without any rational cause. Trust is a key element to a healthy relationship. When this is lacking (particularly when it is lacking without any rational cause), it leads to a lot of arguments and strife within the relationship. You may find yourself walking on eggshells just to make sure your partner can find no cause to distrust you.

➢ Disloyalty: narcissists are especially prone to having affairs. This is even more the case with amorous narcissists as well as unprincipled and elitist narcissists. This is often because they require so much extra attention and validation that they seek it outside of the relationship as well as within it. A cheating partner has been the ruin of many relationships but it is a particularly difficult issue to work through when your partner lacks the capacity to feel guilty about his or her actions.

➤ Unsatisfied needs: because narcissists have difficulty with empathy, they are often inattentive to the needs of their partner. You will find yourself unable to obtain the emotional support you should be getting out of the relationship. When you compound this with the unrealistic demands your partner has for you; the relationship will become emotionally draining rather than fulfilling and enjoyable.

➤ Lack of respect: particularly if your partner is an elitist narcissist, you may feel that he or she does not respect you. Your partner might be excessively condescending or demeaning toward you. He or she will also fail to recognize or praise your achievements. Instead, your partner will act superior and treat you as if you are inferior and owe him or her your affection by virtue of this superiority. Like trust, respect helps form the foundation of a strong relationship. Without respect for each other as individuals, it is difficult to cultivate love and compassion.

> Lack of intimacy: while you may be able to maintain a healthy sex life with your narcissistic partner, intimacy in other ways will be difficult to achieve. Narcissists do not open up emotionally since doing so would risk exposing the vulnerability and inferiority that they refuse to acknowledge within themselves. Even if you take the initiative by opening up and making yourself vulnerable to your partner; this will not be reciprocated. The lack of reciprocation will leave you feeling exposed and isolated.

> Emotional instability: narcissists often experience dramatic mood swings. When your partner wakes up in the morning, you can never be sure whether it will be a good day or a bad day. His or her mood could change dramatically over the course of the day without any rational cause. Living with such instability and unpredictability is difficult and can have a strong influence on your own emotional wellbeing.

Many of these problems can also occur in relationships where neither partner suffers from narcissistic personality disorder. The key difference is that a narcissist will have much more difficulty addressing these issues in a calm and rational way. In fact, a narcissistic partner will be hardly willing to acknowledge that these problems exist at all since he or she will feel entitled to all the benefits of the relationship without feeling any need to contribute.

Each of these problems can exist in varying levels of severity. If your partner is a narcissist, you are likely experiencing many—or even all—of them. When the problems are still relatively mild, it is possible to work through them if you do so carefully and if you feel that your partner and the relationship you have with him or her is worth saving. However, in their most extreme forms, these problems can become toxic and dangerous. In the next chapter, you will read about some warning signs that the relationship has become too toxic.

Chapter 4: Warning Signs

As unfortunate as it is, there is a certain point at which a relationship becomes too toxic. No matter how much you may love the person, it is time to end the relationship and move on so that you can find real happiness in your life. While milder forms of the narcissistic personality disorder have the potential to be dealt with and resolved; severe forms are often too far gone and the risk of staying with the person become too great.

Below are some warning signs that it may be time to get out of a toxic relationship with a narcissistic partner. If after all this, you are still unsure, you should consult a psychiatrist specializing in narcissistic personality disorder to discuss your relationship and seek his or her professional opinion about what you should do.

The Key Warning Signs

➢ Pathological lying: because narcissists often use manipulation in order to get the admiration they desire, they will often tell any lie they think will help them achieve that end goal. If your partner is lying consistently about important and trivial things, your relationship has no foundation in anything real. You cannot trust anything that they say, including when they tell you that they love you. If you cannot trust your partner, you have nothing to build on. This can approach dangerous extremes especially if your partner is having affairs. You will be at an increased risk for STDs if they sleep around and do not use protection.

➢ Fits of anger or rage: narcissists have a hair trigger. The slightest criticism or disagreement can spark an onslaught of abusive language and anger. When the fit of rage is over, your partner will act is if nothing had happened. He or she will show no sign of remorse and if they do apologize, it will not be genuine. It is unhealthy for you to endure such emotional abuse and it can have major consequences in the long term. In some cases the verbal abuse can even become physical. Whether or not it has reached that point in your own relationship, it is time to get out if you are experiencing any form of abuse from your partner.

➢ Manipulative behavior: the person you love should not be doing anything to manipulate you. Period. Strong relationships are built on honesty and trust. You should be able to trust that the things your partner says and does for you are genuine and come from a place of love and not a place of narcissistic selfishness. This manipulative behavior can sometimes fool you into believing that your partner does genuinely care about and love you but you have to try to look past what you want to see and find out what really lies at the root of your partner's actions. If you find yourself doing things you would not normally do or doing things that later make you feel guilty or unhappy just because your partner wants you to; this is manipulation. No matter how much your partner may say he or she loves you; people do *not* manipulate the people they love. You should never be forced into doing something you are not comfortable doing for a loved one.

➢ Feeling obligated: It is a bad sign if you are doing things (like staying in the relationship) simply because you feel obligated to or fear the consequences of not doing them. In a healthy relationship, partners do things for each other because they love each other and because they genuinely wish to see the other person happy. Of course, there are certain responsibilities and duties to uphold in the maintenance of a relationship. But this is different than a sense of obligation. If you are worried that your partner will abandon you or experience a fit of rage unless you do exactly what he or she wants; this is a sign that you are not doing it because you genuinely wish to see him or her happy but, rather, because you do *not* wish to see him or her *un*happy.

➢ Feeling afraid: Just as you should not do things for your partner out of a sense of obligation, you should also not do things out of a sense of fear. Healthy relationships should provide a safe space for both your partner and you. Being with the person should make you feel secure and happy. Feelings of fear should not ever enter the equation. You should not have to fear the person you love.

➢ Becoming isolated from others: narcissists are often extremely jealous. Your partner will become more and more controlling of who you spend your time with and how much time you spend outside of his controlling reach. You will find yourself spending more and more time at home and growing distant from your friends and social circle. This isolation can make you feel unnecessarily dependent upon your partner; as if leaving him or her will mean being utterly alone. Becoming isolated from your social support is dangerous. If your partner does begin abusing, your friends and family may have no idea what is going on. So if you begin to notice that you have grown apart from your friends and family because of your partner, you need to leave. Your loved ones will be there for you. You will not be alone.

➢ Ignoring your own needs: if keeping your partner happy means neglecting or wholly ignoring your own needs, this is not healthy. A relationship should be about give and take with both partners providing emotional support for each other. Someone who loves you will not require you to put aside your own needs in order to appease them because they will have genuine concern for your needs just as you have for theirs. Never allow your own needs and desires to go unmet for the sake of your partner. This sort of relationship cannot end in happiness and will become extremely emotionally draining.

How to End a Relationship with a Narcissist

If you can identify any or all of these warning signs in your own relationship; it is essential that you find the strength to cut ties and walk away. Your partner's happiness should never have to come at the expense of your own. Ending this toxic relationship as soon as possible will allow you the freedom to heal and find someone with whom you can be genuinely happy and experience the full (and wonderful) benefits of a loving relationship.

Ending any relationship is difficult but ending a relationship with a narcissist comes with additional problems. So if you are having trouble figuring out how to approach this problem, here are few tips on how to get out of a toxic relationship with a narcissist:

> Go to therapy: as mentioned earlier, if you are feeling unsure or undecided about your relationship, you should consult a therapist to talk about the problems you are experiencing. They can advise you on how best to approach the problem. Additionally, they can provide an invaluable source of support and reinforcement as you work through the

grueling process of escaping this unhealthy relationship with a narcissist. If you can't afford therapy sessions, find a support group. There are many out there and they can help you not only get professional advice but also find other people who have experienced many of the problems you are experiencing. Learning from others experiences is a great way to figure out how to tackle your own problems.

➢ Do not be afraid to rely on your support system: whether it's your therapist, your support group, your family, your friends, or some combination of these; they are there to help you through this. You do not have to go through this difficult process alone. These are people who love and care about you and want nothing more than to see you happy. Let them help you in this time of need. They know as well as you that when you are in a better place, you will be more than willing to do the same for them. If you feel that you do not really have a support system, make one. Reach out to old friends with whom you have lost touch. Reach out to your family. Find support groups for people who are in your situation. No matter how alone you may feel at this moment or how scared you are of a future without your narcissistic partner; you are *not* alone.

➤ Do not give in to manipulation or abuse: when you finally confront your partner and say that it is time to end the relationship, he or she will likely go to great lengths to discourage you. Your partner may try to manipulate you into staying or use fear to break down your courage. He or she might try to disrupt your everyday life as you are trying to heal from the break up. Instead of falling for these tricks; understand that each one is another sign that you have done the right thing and that all you need to do now is be vigilant and allow time and your social support system to heal you and build your strength back up. Each time you resist these attempts at tricking you, you will grow a little stronger and next time it will be a little easier. Reward yourself for each time that you make it through without giving in.

➢ Learn as much as you can about narcissistic personality disorder: knowledge is your most powerful weapon in this situation. The more you know about how a narcissist operates; the better prepared you are to deal with whatever he or she may throw your way. Also, the more you learn about the disorder; the more you will realize how much of your relationship was built on deceit and manipulation. Realizing that there was no actual love coming from your partner helps motivate you to stay away from him or her. It will also help you avoid falling for another narcissist in the future.

➢ Cut off all contact with your ex-partner: this is easier said than done as your former partner will likely seek you out and try to contact you. However, it is important that you do not initiate any contact and when he or she forces contact; keep it as short as possible and get out of there. If you are having trouble cutting contact, stay with someone who can help you. Let someone else answer your phone or the door. If you are at work, ask a trusted coworker to ask him to leave or call security. If it begins to worsen to dangerous levels (such as threats or harassment), file for a restraining order.

➢ Start a journal: this tip may seem like its coming out of left field but it is also important. You need to make sure to process your feelings during every step of the process. Write in this journal daily. Keeping a journal will help you to deal with what you are experiencing. It will also help you to track your progress. You can read through past entries and notice yourself becoming stronger and stronger even if it doesn't feel like it yet. It can also help to keep a journal about how the relationship was with your partner. Describe in as many details as possible how bad it was so that if you later find yourself tempted to go back to your partner, you can read these and remember just how unhappy and unfulfilled you were.

➢ Get rid of every reminder of your former partner: those little mementos around your home that remind you of him or her can make you feel nostalgic and start missing your partner. It will also cause you to think about your former partner on a near-constant basis. Removing these reminders from your home will also help solidify the feeling that he or she is really gone from your life and the healing process can begin to work faster.

➢ Start doing things for yourself again: all that time catering to every need and desire of your narcissistic partner likely left you with little time to pursue your own interests. This can make you lose your sense of self. Pick up an old hobby you used to enjoy or learn a new skill you have always wanted to learn. Did you dream of one day speaking French? Now's the time to do it. This will not only help you regain your sense of identity apart from your former narcissistic partner, it will also help take your mind off of things. Most importantly, it will help you build up a sense of self-worth that is not connected to your former partner. Pursuing your own interests allows you to become the person you want to be. Not to mention, it

will give you a chance to meet new people
and begin the next chapter of your life.

➢ Allow yourself to grieve: do not spend all
your time distracting yourself and
avoiding your feelings. You need to let
yourself grieve; to let your emotions out.
If you are afraid of being alone during the
grieving process; stay with a trusted
friend or family member, someone with
whom you will feel safe in expressing your
emotions. If you try to avoid feeling this
grief now, the pressure will build and
build until it explodes later in unhealthy
ways. It is ok to feel upset, angry, guilty,
or anything else you feel. Just make sure
you allow yourself to feel it and, more
importantly, to feel it in a safe and
nurturing space where you can work
through your emotions and heal.

It is a difficult process. No one will tell you it is
going to be easy. But you will become a stronger

and happier person for it. So gather up all the strength you have and allow yourself to finally get out of this toxic relationship and find true love and happiness in your life.

Chapter 5: How to Live with a Narcissist

When your relationship has not reached such a toxic point and you don't really see any severe warning signs, there may be hope for saving the relationship. There are treatments and techniques for managing narcissistic personality disorder. These will be discussed in more detail in the next chapter. Here we will discuss strategy you yourself can use to live with a narcissist and help them overcome this personality disorder so that you can have a loving and nurturing relationship with each other.

So, if your relationship has not yet reached its critical breaking point, here are some things you can try in order to make life with your partner more enjoyable and satisfying for the both of you.

> ➢ Identify the problem: if you are reading this book, you have already begun to work on this step. Look for the key traits that

characterize a narcissist and decide if those apply to your partner. Then, read more about narcissistic personality disorder so that you understand not only the symptoms but the causes and treatment options. Learn as much as you can and then look for more to learn. Realize that this is a real problem that needs to be addressed.

➤ Do not be an enabler: once you know what the problem is and how the narcissistic personality disorder operates; you will be better prepared to deal with it. If you notice your partner acting in a narcissistic way (i.e.- acting arrogant, self-absorbed, or ignoring your needs and feelings), confront the problem rather than allowing it to continue or catering to it. Even if it seems easier at the time to just let it go; doing so will only allow the problem to become worse until it is too late and you have no option but to get out or suffer.

➢ Set firm boundaries: since narcissists tend to put their own needs before anyone else's, it is likely that your needs are beginning to fall by the wayside. You need to stop this process dead in its tracks. First, learn to distinguish between the legitimate needs and desires your partner has and the delusional or unrealistic ones. Then make it very clear for your partner what they can and cannot demand from you. Tread carefully here since narcissists are overly sensitive to criticism. Make sure to point out that you do love your partner and that you are willing to meet his or her needs. But *only* when those needs are genuine and realistic. You also need to make it clear that you expect the same in return from your partner.

➢ Avoid one-sided conversations: narcissists have difficulties with empathy and, if allowed, will steer every conversation into a discussion about themselves. They only want to talk about their needs and desires. While it is important to let your partner express his or her needs and desires, it is equally important that you have the space to express yours as well. If the conversation starts to become predominantly about your partner, balance it out and bring it back to yourself so that it becomes a two-sided conversation.

➢ Avoid blaming yourself: narcissists can be manipulative and may make you feel guilty for not allowing them to indulge in their narcissistic behaviors. Do not, on any account, allow yourself to feel guilty or blame yourself. Point out that your needs are also important. Explain that you respect his or her needs but that this relationship needs to be a give and take. If he or she really struggles with empathy, set out clear guidelines for how he or she can practice empathy. Do not play into their attempts at making you feel guilty.

➢ Avoid anger: in arguments, it is easy to become angry very quickly. This is particularly the case with narcissists who tend to fly off the handle quickly. When one person in an argument is angry, it makes the other one angry. Try to resist this and remain calm. Understand that this anger is coming from your partner's inability to healthily deal with conflict. If you also get angry, it will only make your partner angrier and less capable of rationally dealing with the issue. Maintain calm so that you can maintain control of the situation. The more often your partner sees that you maintain calm even in these arguments; the more he or she will realize that you are not going to lose control of the situation or back down from your position no matter what they do.

➢ Get professional help: this is absolutely essential. Unless you are a trained therapist or psychiatrist yourself, you cannot deal with narcissistic personality disorder on your own. If your partner is unwilling to see a therapist—since doing so would mean acknowledging that he or she has a problem, something a narcissist cannot do—suggest couples therapy and frame the problem as a relationship issue rather than strictly an issue with your partner. As you work through couples therapy, your partner will likely grow more and more willing to seek one-on-one therapy where he or she will be able to dig deeper down to the root of the problem. Furthermore, couples therapy can help provide you a safe space to address your issues with your partner. With a trained therapist in the room, it will be easier to keep control of the situation because the therapist will know how to handle your narcissistic partner.

Chapter 6: Managing and Treating Narcissistic Personality Disorder

There are a variety of ways to treat or manage narcissistic personality disorder. Unfortunately, none of these are 100% guaranteed to work and many of them depend upon the person suffering from narcissistic personality disorder being willing to cooperate with the treatment process.

Ideally, your partner will be willing to go to therapy. Long term, out-patient therapy is the best method for treating narcissistic personality disorder provided your partner takes it seriously. Typically the therapy will be combined with medication to help alleviate the most severe symptoms.

While there are no medications on the market specifically designed to treat narcissistic personality disorder, many people benefit from the medications that are used to treat other disorders. Antidepressants help tackle the underlying feelings of inferiority and shame. Antipsychotics help alleviate paranoia and delusional thoughts. Finally, mood stabilizers help stop the unpredictable fluctuations between extremes of highs and lows.

There are two different therapeutic approaches that are typically used when treating narcissistic personality disorder. Sometimes, a third method is used which combines elements from these main two approaches.

The first approach was developed by Otto Kernberg. He advocated for deep analysis of the defensive mechanisms the individual has built up. By showing how these behaviors are, in fact, defensive mechanisms and attempting to illuminate what exactly the individual is using them for (i.e.- the subconscious thought patterns that have resulted in the need for these mechanisms); it is thought that the person suffering from the disorder will grow more self aware and be better able to address the real problems he or she is dealing with.

In the second approach, developed by Heinz Kohut, almost the opposite technique is used. Kohut thought it was better to encourage the narcissistic behaviors and promote the individual's sense of importance. It was his thought that by encouraging it further, the individual would eventually internalize the self-esteem he or she exhibits thereby replacing the feelings of inferiority that had originally lingered in his or her subconscious.

No one has been shown to be consistently more effective than the other. A therapist must decide on a case by case basis which approach would likely work best. In addition to these one-on-one therapy methods, there is group therapy.

Group therapy was originally thought to be out of the question for people suffering from narcissistic personality disorder. It was a reasonable thought considering group therapy usually requires the ability to empathize and be patient while others discuss their issues (skills which narcissists notoriously lack).

However, studies have shown that group therapy can be effective in treating narcissistic personality disorder by helping them to cultivate these important skills. It also helps them become able to feel safe in discussing such vulnerable issues in front of others; making them ultimately more capable of trust. It also helps them realize that they can build fulfilling relationships with others without placing unrealistic demands for admiration and attention.

In severe cases, hospitalization may be necessary. Since your partner is unlikely to recognize this need him or herself; it will be up to you to look out for the signs that your partner needs to be hospitalized. Essentially, hospitalization becomes necessary when:

a) Your partner becomes a danger to him or herself

b) Your partner becomes a danger to you or others

c) Your partner is unable to take care of even his or her most basic needs without help.

Hospitalization may also be necessary for those who are entirely unwilling to go to out-patient therapy on their own.

Your partner's time in the hospital can help him or her realize how serious the issue has become and that he or she really should take treatment seriously and try to get help. The intensive treatment he or she will receive will go a long way in preparing your partner for the reality that he or she needs to take therapy seriously. After the staff at the hospital determines that your partner can return home, make sure that he or she continues out-patient treatment (either one-on-one therapy, group therapy or a combination of both).

For your part, there are ways that you can manage your partner's narcissistic personality disorder while he or she receives professional help from a therapist. Making sure you are prepared to manage it at home will help ensure that your partner's progress continues even when he or she is not in therapy.

Here are some ways to manage a narcissistic personality disorder:

> Remain calm: with your partner receiving therapy, it is more important than ever that you remain calm when dealing with him or her. Your partner's psyche is going to be especially fragile at this point and he or she may fluctuate widely between trying to resort back to their old behaviors and becoming extremely vulnerable. Do not let yourself lose hope or control when

your partner appears to relapse back into old habits. Take a deep breath and maintain control. It always gets worse before it gets better. As long as your partner is continuing to go his or her therapy sessions, you should stay hopeful.

➢ Be supportive: as your partner attempts to venture further and further into such unknown territory as acknowledging his or her real needs and emotions; he or she is going to be particularly vulnerable. You want to make sure that you create a safe space for your partner and make it clear that you are there to provide support and he or she can safely confide in you.

➢ Be wary of false signs of recovery: remember that your partner suffers from narcissistic personality disorder. He or she may try to manipulate you into believe he or she is getting better when, in fact, that is not true. To help you stay abreast of these false signs, you may want to seek therapy yourself. Talking to a therapist— especially the same therapist that is treating your partner—will help you stay aware of the process and learn to distinguish deceit from real progress in your partner.

➤ Be patient: the issues and feelings that are at the root of narcissistic personality disorder take time to resolve. Be patient with your partner and understand that he or she is not going to be cured overnight. Learn to recognize and appreciate the small steps your partner is making in the right direction.

➤ Understand the treatment process: while doctor-patient confidentiality prevents you from knowing exactly what the treatment process entails for your partner; you should at least know what kind of therapeutic methods are being used. Furthermore, if your partner has been prescribed medications, make sure that you read the information on these medications thoroughly. Understand their side effects and what other drugs they interact poorly with. You may also want to keep track of the medication and make sure that your partner is taking it as prescribed.

➢ Know when it is time to get out: unfortunately, therapy does not work for everyone. This is especially the case for people who refuse to take it seriously and make use of their treatment. If your partner is stubborn and refusing to get better; the problems you are currently experiencing are only going to get worse. Get out before you get hurt.

Treatments can go a long way in helping your partner deal with the issues causing the narcissistic symptoms. But your partner must be receptive to treatment. Try to encourage him or her throughout the process and, above all, be as supportive as possible without enabling his narcissistic behaviors. And always be aware of the warning signs and know when the relationship has become too toxic. You are not obligated to stay with your partner if you feel unsafe or unhappy with him or her. And do not blame yourself for wanting to leave. You have no reason to feel guilty. Your happiness matters, too.

Conclusion

This book is intended only as a guide to help you navigate the complex and difficult reality of living with a narcissist. You should not use it to actually diagnose your partner. Only a licensed psychiatrist can accurately identify what is troubling your partner.

However, it is just as important that you prepare yourself for dealing with your partner's narcissistic personality disorder as it is for your partner to finally realize that he or she needs help.

Above all, it is the hope of this author that this guide can help you feel a little less loss and overwhelmed about your current situation. There are resources and options out there for you. Do not be afraid to seek out help.

Reading through this guide is a great first step in dealing with your partner's narcissistic personality disorder. You are now better informed about what you are facing and how you can manage it. Continue researching further into the issue and find out what resources are available to you in your area.

Finally, stay cautious of the warning signs described in chapter 5 of this book. When the problems in a relationship involving a narcissist persist; they can worsen to the point that it becomes too risky for you to stay. Furthermore, you should not stay in a relationship that is dissatisfying or emotionally draining when you would be better off getting out there and finding a partner that would better be able to give you the love and respect which you deserve.

Be strong and don't be afraid to do what will ultimately make you happy!